GALE
CENGAGE Learning

Poetry for Students, Volume 14

Staff

Editor: Anne Marie Hacht.

Contributing Editors: Michael L. LaBlanc, Ira Mark Milne, Jennifer Smith, Daniel Toronto, Carol Ullmann.

Managing Editor, Content: Dwayne D. Hayes.

Managing Editor, Product: David Galens.

Publisher, Literature Product: Mark Scott.

Literature Content Capture: Joyce Nakamura, *Managing Editor*. Madeline Harris, *Associate Editor*.

Research: Victoria B. Cariappa, *Research Manager*. Sarah Genik, Ron Morelli, Tamara Nott, Tracie A. Richardson, *Research Associates*. Nicodemus Ford, *Research Assistant*.

Permissions: Maria Franklin, *Permissions*

Manager. Shalice Shah-Caldwell, *Permissions Associate.*

Manufacturing: Mary Beth Trimper, *Manager, Composition and Electronic Prepress.* Evi Seoud, *Assistant Manager, Composition Purchasing and Electronic Prepress.* Stacy Melson, *Buyer.*

Imaging and Multimedia Content Team: Barbara Yarrow, *Manager.* Randy Bassett, *Imaging Supervisor.* Robert Duncan, Dan Newell, Luke Rademacher, *Imaging Specialists.* Pamela A. Reed, *Imaging Coordinator.* Leitha Etheridge-Sims, Mary Grimes, David G. Oblender, *Image Catalogers.* Robyn V. Young, *Project Manager.* Dean Dauphinais, *Senior Image Editor.* Kelly A. Quin, *Image Editor.*

Product Design Team: Pamela A. E. Galbreath, *Senior Art Director.* Michael Logusz, *Graphic Artist.*

agency, institution, publication, service, or individual does not imply endorsement of the editors or publisher. Errors brought to the attention of the publisher and verified to the satisfaction of the publisher will be corrected in future editions.

This publication is a creative work fully protected by all applicable copyright laws, as well as by misappropriation, trade secret, unfair competition, and other applicable laws. The authors and editors of this work have added value to the underlying factual material herein through one or more of the following: unique and original selection, coordination, expression, arrangement, and classification of the information.

Incident in a Rose Garden

Donald Justice 1967

Introduction

Donald Justice included "Incident in a Rose Garden" in his 1967 collection of poems, *Night Light*, and revised the poem for his *Selected Poems*, published by Atheneum, in 1979. Unlike most of Justice's other poems, "Incident in a Rose Garden" tells a story. The three characters, the Gardener, the Master, and Death, play out a familiar scene in which Death, whom Justice describes in stereotypical fashion as adorned in black and being "thin as a scythe," mistakes the identity of one character for another. The language is simple, yet formal, the dialogue straightforward, the theme clear: Death may come when least expected; live life with that thought in mind. Other themes addressed include the relationship of human beings to nature, self-deception, and fate versus self-creation. In its use of stock characters and situation and its obvious moral, the poem resembles a medieval allegory.

In the revised version of "Incident in a Rose Garden," Justice moves from an objective point of view, which contains only the dialogue of the characters, to a first person point of view in which the Master relates the story. This change allows for a more detailed description of the Gardener and Death and gives the surprise ending more bite. The relationship between a consciousness of death and an appreciation of life is a theme in Wallace Stevens's poetry, which Justice notes as a primary influence on his own writing. Justice dedicates the poem to poet Mark Strand who, like Justice, writes about the presence of death in everyday life and the ways in which the self responds to and is shaped by that presence. Strand was a student of Justice's at the University of Iowa.

Author Biography

Donald Rodney Justice was born in Miami, Florida, in 1925 to Vascoe J., a carpenter, and Mary Ethel Cook Justice, both of whom had moved to Florida from Georgia in the early 1920s. His mother encouraged Justice's interest in the arts early in his life, providing him with piano lessons, and Justice has remained passionate about music and art throughout his life. In Miami, Justice studied with composer Carl Ruggles, one of the first professional artists he ever met, and poet George Marion O'Donnell, who taught him how to read poets such as Thomas Hardy in a new way. After earning his bachelor's degree in English from the University of Miami, Justice moved to New York City for a year before resuming his studies at the University of North Carolina at Chapel Hill, where he earned a master's degree in 1947. Although enrolled in Stanford's doctoral program for a year, Justice felt the pace of the program was too slow. He left to study in the Writing Workshop at the University of Iowa, where he received his Ph. D. in 1954. As student and teacher, Justice has worked with many well-known writers including Yvor Winters, Robert Lowell, William Logan, Karl Shapiro, and Charles Wright. One of his students at Iowa, Mark Strand, to whom Justice dedicates "Incident in a Rose Garden," was poet laureate for the United States from 1990 to 1992.

Justice is known as a technician of poetry, an

accomplished technician who describes himself as "a rationalist defender of the meters." His work is as much influenced by William Carlos Williams as by Wallace Stevens. Though critics sometimes fault his poetry for being too restrained, Justice has developed a reputation as a craftsman who has influenced a good number of younger poets. His poetic output has not been prolific, but it has been steady. His poetry collections include *The Summer Anniversaries* (1960), *Night Light* (1967), *Departures* (1973), and *Selected Poems* (1979). Justice's collection of prose and poetry, *The Sunset Maker: Poems/Stories/A Memoir*, was published in 1987, and his collection of essays, *Oblivion: On Writers and Writing* came out in 1998. In addition to writing poems, Justice has edited a number of books, including *The Collected Poems of Weldon Kees* and *Contemporary French Poetry*, and has written a libretto *The Death of Lincoln*. His awards include a Rockefeller Foundation fellow in poetry, Lamont Poetry Award, a Ford Foundation fellowship in theater, National Endowment for the Arts grants, a Guggenheim fellowship, and the Pulitzer Prize in poetry for *Selected Poems*. A professor for most of his adult life, Justice retired from the University of Florida in 1992.

Title

The title of the poem makes use of understatement in the same way as the poem. By titling the poem "Incident in a Rose Garden" instead of, for example, "Death Visits the Master," Justice creates a sense of mystery, of suspense. Readers are never told directly the significance of what is happening but must make the connections themselves. Setting the poem in a rose garden underscores the relationships among death, nature, and human beings and shows the folly of human beings in thinking that they are somehow not a part of the natural world, which includes death.

Gardener

In the first stanza of "Incident in a Rose Garden," the Gardener addresses his Master, telling him that he "encountered Death" in the garden. The Gardener recognized him "through his pictures," meaning the stereotypical ways that death has been personified in painting and illustrations: all in black and "thin as a scythe." This description evokes death's identity as the grim reaper. A scythe is an instrument with a long blade used to cut crops or grass. It belongs in a garden. The personification of death, however, is as old as hu-mankind and forms a part of every culture. The image of Death's wide-open mouth evokes the devouring void, the very nothingness that comes with the cessation of consciousness. His teeth are predatory, and the end rhymes of "open / spoken" have a hypnotic effect. The formality of the Gardener's language belies his experience. Readers wouldn't expect someone who just encountered death to respond with such a restrained tone. It is this restraint, however, helped by the formal restraint of three-line stanzas and three-beat lines, that gives the poem its shape.

Media Adaptations

- Watershed Tapes distributes an audiocassette of Justice reading his poems, titled *Donald Justice: "Childhood" & Other Poems* (1985).

- The audiocassettes *Donald Justice I & II* were released in 1984 and 1989 by New Letters on the Air.

- The Archive of Recorded Poetry and Literature, Washington, D.C., has audiotapes of Justice reading with Betty Adcock on March 21, 1989.

- The Archive of Recorded Poetry and Literature, Washington, D.C., has audiotapes of Justice reading with Eavan Boland on October 15, 1992.

The Gardener relates his fear that Death had come for him. Readers can infer that he is quitting because he believes that he has only a short time to live. It is common for people, when told they are going to die, to put their affairs in order and to prioritize what is important to them. The Gardener wants to see his sons and to see California before he dies, which are understandable desires. The introduction of California, however, seems anachronistic for this poem, whose word choice and setting seem to predate the discovery of the New World. In this instance, California is a promised land, an exotic place of fantasy, which readers can assume the Gardener has thought about visiting before.

Master

In between dialogue, readers can assume that the Master went to the rose garden to see Death, from whom his Gardener had run. Although the Master addresses Death as "Sir," as his Gardener had addressed him, his words suggest a restrained anger. He accuses Death, whom he refers to as a "stranger," of "threatening" his Gardener, and warns him off his property, which is ironic since Death has the final say over who and what gets to live in the rose garden. The Master assumes an adversarial stance towards Death, treating him as an intruder when he tells him, "I welcome only friends here." The Master's restraint is heightened by the end rhyme of all of his lines.

Topics for Further Study

- Interview your classmates, family, and friends about a time when they had a premonition of death. What similarities do you see in their stories?

- Justice dedicated this poem to poet Mark Strand. Read Strand's collection of poems *Darker*. Discuss similarities between the two poets' representation and awareness of death.

- Brainstorm a list of ways in which death is visually represented in contemporary art, film, writing, and culture. What gender is death? How old? Where and when does death usually appear? What can you conclude from these facts about society's relationship with death?

- Research what happens to the brain in the last minutes before death. Report your findings to your class.

- Research the stories of those who have had near-death experiences. How have these people changed their lives as a result of the experience?

- If you were told that you were going to die tomorrow, how would you spend your last day? Make an itinerary, right down to your last minute.

- Continue the poem, writing one or two three-line stanzas in which the master replies to death. Then write another stanza or two in which Death responds. Try to get as close to Justice's tone and style as possible.

Death

Death responds to the Master, telling him, ironically, that he was a friend of his father. Readers can deduce from this that the Master's father is dead. Again, the use of such understatement, a feature of the poem as a whole, is part of the formal speech of the characters and belies the significance of what is actually happening. When Death tells the Master that the reason the Gardener was afraid was that "Old men mistake my gestures," he means that older people live closer to death, believing that it may come at any moment.

In the last three lines of the poem, readers learn that Death's intention for coming to the rose garden was not to take the Gardener but to take the Master. This reversal is an example of situational irony, in which there is a contradiction between expectation and reality.

Death

"Incident in a Rose Garden" underscores the arrogance of human beings and how they mistakenly assume they are beyond the rules and processes of the natural world. The relationship between the Gardener and the Master parallels the relationship between the Master and Death. In the first relationship, the Gardener treats his Master with the deference and civility of an inferior, even though he quits his job. He comes running to the Master after he sees Death in the garden. The Master, believing that Death has come for the Gardener, in his arrogance refuses to recognize Death's power, calling him a "stranger" and telling him he is not welcome. He assumes that, because he is the owner of the rose garden, he owns death as well and can order him about the same way he orders his servants about. Such hubris is common for many who see themselves as existing separate from the natural world. Many religions warn against making oneself into a god. In the Bible, for example, Proverbs 16.18 says, "Pride goes before destruction, / and a haughty spirit before a fall." Proud human beings sometimes believe that the world somehow exists for them and not the other way around. Death's response to the Master, his measured coolness, and his own extension of "friendship" show who the real Master is, and

Death, quite literally, puts the Master in his place.

Nature

The fact that Death appears in the rose garden underscores the place of death in the order of the natural world. He not only encounters the Gardener there but the Master as well, emphasizing that death's dominion is nature itself. A rose garden is a place of great beauty, but that beauty is seasonal. When the season changes, the roses wither and die. So, too, with human beings. Justice, however, shows how death can come unexpectedly and out of season. Although the Gardener is older than his Master and thinks that Death has come for him, in fact, Death has come for the younger man. A rose garden is also a cultivated place, man-made, ordered to human desire. Death's appearance upsets that order, suggesting that humanity's attempt to control nature, like the Master's attempt to order Death out of his garden, is doomed to fail. Death's confidence in the face of the Master's impoliteness, highlights this.

Style

Narrative

"Incident in a Rose Garden" is a dramatized narrative poem. Narrative poems are stories, with characters, a plot, and action, as opposed to lyric poems, which are the utterance of one speaker, often describing or explaining an emotion or thought. This poem is all dialogue and is presented from an objective point of view. This means that the narrator never intrudes to comment on the action or to explain or describe what is happening. In this way, the poem resembles a very short play. Readers have to infer from the dialogue the theme of the story. The organization of the poem into three-line stanzas, whose lines have three beats apiece, makes the work look and sound like a poem.

Personification

When ideas or inanimate things are given human qualities, they are personified. Justice personifies death by drawing on traditional depictions of death and by packing his description with symbolic imagery appropriate to the idea of death. He is dressed in black and is "thin as a scythe" and his mouth "stood open. /... with white teeth"—all images we associate with the grim reaper, a popular depiction of death. The Gardener and the Master obviously cannot be personifications, but they do represent two very different social strata.

Historical Context

The time period of "Incident in a Rose Garden" isn't explicit, though its themes, structure, and diction suggest the Middle Ages. Justice's poem evokes the idea of *danse macabre*, or the dance of death, a notion that grew out of Western Europe's response to the bubonic plague, which killed millions of people beginning in the fourteenth century. In paintings and poems, the allegorical concept of danse macabre depicted a procession of people from all walks of life, both living and dead. One of the earliest representations of the dance of death is in a series of paintings (1424–1425) formerly in the Cimetière des Innocents, a cemetery in Paris that was moved in the eighteenth century. These paintings depict a procession of living people from the church and state being led to their graves by corpses and skeletons. The living are arranged according to their rank so as to present an inclusive representation of humanity. This scene is meant to underscore the leveling power of death and the idea that death can come at any time. The earliest use of the term danse macabre occurs in 1376 in a poem by Jean Le Fevre. The obsession with death also found expression during this time in the morality play. Morality plays were allegories in dramatic form, performed to teach viewers the path from sin to salvation and the fragility of earthly life. Justice's poem does not include a procession like the dance of death, but it does include a personification of death and the character types of Master and Gardener, who stand for social classes, and it does emphasize the idea that death does not discriminate based on social status. A few of the more popular morality plays include *Mankind* and *Everyman*.

The rate at which the bubonic plague spread and the fact that no one knew what caused it, created a heightened anxiety and uncertainty. Theories were bandied about, including one put forth by scholars at the University of Paris, who held that a combination of earthquakes and astrological forces were responsible for the plague. Many believed that the plague was God's punishment for humanity's sins and that extreme penitence was required to appease God's wrath. Groups of people known as flagellants paraded through towns whipping themselves and criticizing the Catholic Church for not following God's law. Jews also became the scapegoat for the disease, as people frantically sought someone to blame for the epidemic. Thousands of Jews were persecuted and slaughtered by hysterical mobs during this time.

In the mid-1960s, when this poem was written, the United States was becoming more deeply involved with the war in Vietnam. Televised images of the war, including footage of dead soldiers, became a staple of the nightly news. In 1968, shortly after the Tet offensive, American photographer Eddie Adams caught a South Vietnamese security official on film executing a Viet Cong prisoner.

Compare & Contrast

- **1967:** The life expectancy for Americans is 70.5 years.

  Today: The life expectancy for Americans is almost 77 years.

- **1967:** International Treaty bans weapons of mass destruction from space, and the United Nations approves a nuclear non-proliferation treaty.

  Today: Arguing that rogue states could still compromise the United States security and put millions of citizens at risk during a nuclear attack, the Bush administration argues for continuing development on a national missile defense shield.

- **1967:** The World Health Organization begins a program to get rid of the smallpox virus completely, which has killed millions of people in its history. Although the virus had been stamped out in Europe and North America, it still exists in poorer regions of the world. In May 1980, WHO formally announces that smallpox has been eliminated.

  Today: More than 33 million people

worldwide have been infected with the HIV virus, which can lead to Acquired Immunodeficiency Syndrome (AIDS). More than two and one half million people die from the virus.

For Vietnam War protestors, this photograph served as evidence of the brutalities of the war and undermined American assumptions about the South Vietnamese themselves.

The presence of death and mortality is evidenced throughout *Night Light*. In 1965, Justice himself turned forty years old. "Men at Forty," one of the heavily anthologized poems from the collection, describes Justice's sentiment about this milestone, and other poems in the collection address the idea of mortality and aging and of regret for a life unlived.

Critical Overview

The collection in which "Incident in a Rose Garden" appears, *Night Light*, was Justice's second full-length collection and contains some of his best-known works, including "Men at Forty," "The Man Closing Up," and "The Thin Man." Reviewing the collection, Robert Pawlowski stresses that Justice is more than simply a technically brilliant poet but is "a good poet who is as interested in life, death, hate, love, fun, and sorrow as anyone." Noting the sadness of the poems in the volume, William Pritchard was not as flattering, writing that "the best line in the book is an epigraph" from someone else.

In *Shenandoah*, critic Joel Conarroe praises Justice for bringing "a controlled, urbane intensity to his Chekhovian descriptions of loss and the unlived life." Conarroe notes that Justice's poems "are all fairly accessible on one or two careful readings." James McMichael agrees, writing, "Justice is tightly in charge of everything that goes on within his poems, so much so that very few of them are not almost totally accessible after careful reading." William Hunt considers Justice's poem a conservative response to the often hyper-emotionalism of romanticism, writing, "Mr. Justice's poems are eloquent replies in a classical mode to the all or nothing element in romanticism. The best poems in the book are closest to this anachronistic struggle." Such a struggle expectedly contains a barely restrained tension between "message" and form. Richard Howard notes that the collection emits "a kind of vexed buzz close to the fretful."

What Do I Read Next?

- Justice dedicated "Incident in a Rose Garden" to poet, friend, former student, and former Poet Laureate of the United States, Mark Strand. Like Justice, Strand frequently writes about the absence of the self and the sadness of human life. His *Selected Poems* (1979) is a good introduction to his work.

- Philip Ziegler's *The Black Death* (1998) details the plague that gripped Europe from the fourteenth to the seventeenth centuries. Ziegler notes that plague probably cost Europe between 12.5 and 70 percent of its population according to region, population density, hygiene, and other factors.

- Justice's *New and Selected Poems* (1997) updates his Pulitzer Prize-winning 1979 *Selected Poems* by changing the previous volume's selection and adding many poems written in the intervening fifteen years.

Sources

Conarroe, Joel O., "Five Poets," in *Shenandoah*, Vol. 18, No. 4, Summer 1967, pp. 87–88.

Howard, Richard, "Donald Justice," in *Alone with America: Essays on the Art of Poetry in the United States since 1950*, Atheneum, 1980.

Hunt, William, "The Poems of Donald Justice," in *Poetry*, Vol. 112, No. 4, July 1968, pp. 272–73.

Justice, Donald, *A Donald Justice Reader*, Middlebury College Press, 1991.

—, *Night Light*, Wesleyan University Press, 1967.

—, *Oblivion*, Story Line Press, 1998.

—, *Selected Poems*, Atheneum, 1979.

—, ed., *The Collected Poems of Weldon Kees*, Stone Wall Press, 1960.

Justice, Donald, and Alexander Aspel, eds., *Contemporary French Poetry*, University of Michigan Press, 1965.

Malkoff, Karl, *Escape from the Self: A Study in Contemporary American Poetry and Poetics*, Columbia University Press, 1977.

McMichael, James, "Justice," in *North American Review*, Vol. 252, No. 6, November 1967, pp. 39–40.

Pawlowski, Robert, Review of *Night Light*, in

Denver Quarterly, Vol. 2, No. 2, Summer 1967, pp. 175–77.

Pritchard, William H., "Poetry Chronicle," in *Hudson Review*, Vol. 20, No. 2, Summer 1967, pp. 309–10.

Further Reading

Gioia, Dana, "Interview with Donald Justice," in *American Poetry Review*, Vol. 25, No. 1, January/February 1996, p. 37.

> Justice discusses the influence of music on his poetry and comments on the proliferation of creative writing programs.

Gioia, Dana, and William Logan, eds. *Certain Solitudes: On the Poetry of Donald Justice*, University of Arkansas Press, 1998.

> This book collects essays and reviews written on Justice's poetry. It remains the single best source of criticism on the poet.

Howard, Richard, *Alone with America: Essays on the Art of Poetry in the United States since 1950*, Atheneum, 1969.

> This collection of essays on post–World War II American poetry by one of America's most insightful critics is useful for those who want to locate Justice's work among his contemporaries.